A CUMULUS FICTION

poems by

Judith Pacht

Finishing Line Press
Georgetown, Kentucky

A CUMULUS FICTION

ACKNOWLEDGMENTS

My thanks also to these journals which published the poems, some under different titles:

The American Journal of Poetry (Exposed),
Rattle (Unseen),
Spillway (My Walk, My City)
The International Journal NIMROD (A Cumulous Fiction) in their 35th Literary Awards issue.

Publisher: Leah Maines
Editor: Christen Kincaid
Author Photo: Lynn Greenberg
Cover Art and Design: Tania Baban

Printed in the USA on acid-free paper.
Order online: www.finishinglinepress.com
            also available on amazon.com

Author inquiries and mail orders:
Finishing Line Press
P. O. Box 1626
Georgetown, Kentucky 40324
U. S. A.

Table of Contents

for Ken, my heart & home

and in memory of
Dorothy and Edgar Roedelheimer,
Jane Siegel and Jerry Pacht
who taught me to treasure the natural world
and those who live in it

FIRST WORDS

This series began with a game in which each word from a particular *haiku* is arranged sequentially and vertically on the page as the first word in each line of a poem. This way the haiku can be read vertically as well, and so in a way these poems pay homage to the Japanese tradition in which characters are written from top to bottom. A reader might look at my poems as a riff on the contemporary acrostic, and maybe my friend, the poet Richard Garcia did just that when he devised the exercise.

As I wrote them I found myself in conversation with Issa, Basho, Buson, Shiki and others, building as we so often do on the backs of our forbears. I hope my writing responds to their essential wisdom, but when I thought I was finished I was not. The masters' *haiku* still leads me further into conversations with myself.

i.

A sudden shower falls—
and naked I am riding
on a naked horse!

Issa

夕立や裸で乗しはだか馬

A day is a lifetime.
Sudden shadows shift,
shower light on dark. It
falls on sage, spiked cactus.
And the sun falls too, in love with chamisa,
naked, it bends with the wind.
I & the gray-green leaves
am longing for warmth,
riding any light shaft.
On summer days I lie on
a ledge exposed,
naked & alert, curry-combed & sleek as a
horse. Nostrils flared, ready.

ii.

*Mosquito at my ear—
does it think
I'm deaf?*

Issa

年寄と見るや鳴蚊も耳の際

Mosquito wings whine
at or near E flat, remind me of
my self, of what I want to hear. The closed
ear doesn't & the head does. It listens to what
does stroking, ignores the rest—
it is joy & despair, hope & shame. Sometimes I
think the self needs an introduction. A way in.
I'm struggling with that habit, choosing to be
deaf.

iii.

New Year's day—
everything in blossom!
I feel about average.

Issa

目出度さもちう位也おらが春

New says change, a thrill or last
year's terror. Your absence leaves me, the
day empty. *Is anybody?* you'd say.
Everything we counted on gone.
In a life of dirty dishes, unmade beds, one
blossom is meant to bloom forever.
I water every bud, wish it to unfurl.
Feel the thorns below, imagine what petals are
about to be (furled like me.) This day wide open,
average for here. Inside thunderheads.

iv.

Green frog,
is your body also
freshly painted?
Akutagawa

青蛙おのれもペンキぬりたてか

Green canopy shadows leap-
frog, echo what
is: a vault of plane trees arching.
Your vermillion pulse, your
body language. The sonata's coda
also throbs. I miss your scent—
freshly cut sage—what's inside, not
painted skin deep.

v.

Napped half the day;
no one
punished me!

　　　　　　Issa

今までは罰も当たらず昼寝蚊帳

Napped in a reverie,
half noon, half shade.
The sun warms, shadows tease.
Day. Call it an eclipse of spirit.
No permanent night, only flitting fear.
One too-long moment, as if to be
punished for longing or absence.
Me, a black moon.

vi.

Don't weep, insects—
Lovers, stars themselves,
Must part.

                              Issa

鳴な虫別るる恋はほしにさへ

for a sowbug:

Don't regret distance, don't
weep over it. Tiny
insects' life spans shrink by the hour.
Lovers (we careless ones) bend our own sum.
Stars are light years away, they take care of
themselves, whirl orbits far from other galaxies.
Must we? Be done. In other words
part.

vii.

Even in Kyoto—
hearing the cuckoo's cry—
I long for Kyoto.

Basho

京にても京なつかしや時鳥

Even at dawn dreams & daylight marry
in a Murakami world. Our spirit-words walk
Kyoto silently. Yes, & at dusk we tread lightly.
Hearing footsteps might make us disappear.
The past lives inside us here on Shinmonzendori. A
cuckoo's voice calls from the clockshop. No hawkers
cry out, only the shuffle of shoppers shoes—& mine.
I am comfort, I sway under my silks,
long to sing chansons, speak French with the French.
For twenty years I have poured tea, danced, imitated pleasure.
Kyoto, my prison.

viii.

No one travels
along this way but I
this autumn evening.
                    Basho

この道を行く人なしに秋の暮

No snow today, just a cleanswept sky.
One hump of the Manzanos hides the cloud's
travels. Stealthy winds build
along top ridges behind peaks.
This is drama—not knowing the
way, finding a new path.
But danger tries the heart.
I go with the blue north, break
this uncertain weather.
Autumn stops my heart, but one calm
evening restores.

ix.

A summer river being crossed
how pleasing
with sandals in my hands!
                    Buson

夏河を越すうれしさよ手に草履

A dent in the wooden floor.
Summer light hides it & my scar, a white
river of tissue hidden by these gloves.
Being imperfect as gods & gardens is a line
crossed every day. Take this woman in a crate.
How does she spell *home*?
Pleasing, I think checking my reflection: lipstick,
with blush, with shame. While the woman's
sandals keep her cold feet cold.
In misery. I drive the overpass, this
my full, full summer. My scarred hidden
hands.

x.

*Buying leeks
and walking home
under the bare trees.*
                    Buson

葱買て枯木の中を帰りけり

Buying something at market, say
leeks, fills one with promise,
and it's more satisfying than a meal.
Walking lets one embroider on absurdities at
home, obsess over lives & loves hidden
under artful distractions, charades, masks.
The hidden part (richer than leeks & cream, never
bare) says taste changes. Like seasons, like
trees, like you. Unpredictable.

xi.

For you fleas too
the nights must be long,
they must be lonely.

Issa

蚤どもがさぞ夜永だろ淋しかろ

For so long my itch has needed
you, only you, to scratch. But
fleas—they give a little, get a little: saliva, blood.
Too little to worry about losing. Still
the itch.
Nights I miss what was never there.
Must life
be simply virtual? Loneliness
long since has been replaced with basil, garlic, tomatoes.
They must cook down to marmalade. Not
must—they *do*. A sauce covers, but
be honest—underneath, the itch. Yes Issa, at night it's
lonely.

xii.

Lightening flash—
what I thought were faces
are plumes of pampas grass.
Basho

稲妻や顔のところが薄の穂

Lightening: white heat. A weightless
flash—a sudden load lifted.
What lies between them.
I am suspended, hanging, no
thought of time. It's 2 AM. I boil an egg as if it
were morning. It's safe this way. Those white hot
faces (poppies, fragments blowing sideways)
are only my constructions. My fires burst into
plumes into nothing at all. Collisions
of nothingness in my head. Inside fear lies freedom,
pampas grass does swing easily in the breeze. Cut
grass *is* simply grass cut, the scent earthy, the soil wet & sweet.

xiii.

Climb Mount Fuji
O snail,
but slowly, slowly
Issa

かたつぶりそろそろ登れ富士の山

Climb or crawl or barely stir. Some
mount steep slopes as though subduing
Fuji, panther haunches oiled.
O stands for others who wait.
Snail-like they move up
but barely. Imperceptible shifts. Think
slowly. I trip,
slowly recover. Doubt passes for progress.

xiv.

Everything I touch
with tenderness, alas,
pricks like a bramble.
                                    Issa

古里やよるも障も茨の花

Everything she sewed for me
I keep in a case. She saved me—her
touch soft on my neck when I was two.
With her music, trust & safety.
Tenderness was ours, was mine.
Alas, (she'd say), *they just don't know,* & yet
pricks from her smocking needle could wound—
like her tongue.
A stab undeserved, unforeseen. Her barbed
bramble cut deep.

xv.

Even with insects—
some can sing,
some can't.

                    Issa

世
の
中
や
鳴
虫
に
さ
え
上
手
下
手

Even & evening silence falls
with dark over the field.
Insects appear one by one.
Some hobble, some creep.
Can you see—can you speak?
Sing one voice says & warbles Issa's song.
Some of us sing *a cappella,* rub our legs. We who
can't sing, write.

Hell:
Bright autumn moon
pond snails crying
I   *in the saucepan.*

Issa

夕月や鍋の中にて鳴田にし

Hell: someone's kitchen -- knives lined up
bright & shiny, long for a balanced hand. This
autumn evening the heavy air hides an innocent
moon undressing as dawn looks away, but the shallow
pond here holds steady. Fish feed, multiply in shallows.
Snails gorge on sorrel. A possum fears the coyote
crying nearby but slakes his thirst, ignores howls
in easy earshot. Balance again. And wild-caught salmon?
The cook poaches it for her omega oils. Call it denial in a
saucepan.

xvii.

Light of the moon
moves west, flowers' shadows
creep eastward.

            Buson

月光西にわたれば花影東に歩むかな

Light at night sees the unseen underbellies
of rocks, a scramble of millipedes & sowbugs.
The paralyzing exposure. A full
moon paints Rothko on the meadow, blueblack & dancing,
moves the insects from chaos to choreography.
West of the field salt & ocean spray, a lone
flower's mist and bloom. The shadow of
shadows. Deep purples, blackgreens vibrate,
creep into the dim field. Wait—look
eastward—orange light is tricking the night.

xviii.

Autumn wind—
mountain's shadow
wavers.

Issa

秋
風
や
ひ
ょ
ろ
ひ
ょ
ろ
山
の
影
法
師

Autumn & its shifting clouds—and
wind—they break dark promises, lick the
mountain's deep green flanks, a cumulus fiction.
Shadow & light bicker on their bed, passion
wavers.

xix.

Over the wintry
forest, winds howl in rage
with no leaves to blow.
                    Soseki

木枯らしの今や吹くとも散る葉なし

Over & over words fly out,
the same phonics: plosives, fricatives,
wintry *P & Ks, F & Z*s. Remember a place of
forest overgrowth, the kind shade of a vowel
winds never reach. Low enough to
howl a rebuke. We hum
in & around fallen logs. Somewhere
rage eddies but not here.
With winter, the how & why of words.
No residue of fallen memory.
Leaves mulch. Another cycle
to pass along. Whirling *P-Z-Ks*
blow: *full moon.*

XX.

The crow has flown away:
swaying in the evening sun,
a leafless tree.

Soseki

烏飛んで夕日に動く冬木かな

The gate here rings bells to scare off
crow or jay, an uninvited guest. What
has been an early warning
flown awry is meant to keep
away intruders. Frighten them.
Swaying—the slightest movement
in the air wakes up the night. Cowbells.
The triangle. A tambourine. But wait, there's
evening music if you listen, a play of light like
sun at midnight sets off your noonday heat.
A wind sings a symphony. No silent
leafless limbs hang. Bells ring. Not a
tree at all, & once I thought you were ordinary.

NOTES

The intent here is to capture the essence of the *haiku* poet's poem, not to end up with a literal line-by-line rendering. For example the *haiku* (ii) *"mosquito at my ear—/does it think/ I'm deaf?"* in its literal and original form ends with "an old person", but the more playful translation "deaf" makes the same association and meaning but enlarges the poem's scope adding humor and punch.

vii.
Haruki Murakami, Japanese author of *The Wind-up Bird Chronicle* and other surrealist novels.
Shinmonzendori, a narrow street in old Kyoto lined with antique stores. Geishas often walk on Shinmonzendori and adjacent streets in the late afternoon.

xx.
Plosives: In phonetics, a consonant sound is made by closing off part of the oral cavity. These sounds are usually associated with the letters *p, t* and *k; b, d* and *g.* **Fricatives** are characterized by outward pressure from a breath, usually associated with letters such as *f* and *s; v* and *z.*

LAST WORDS

Years ago we wrote what we call *haiku* syllabically, that is in three lines of 5, 7 and 5 syllables each. We were imitating the traditional Japanese *haiku* pattern of 17 *on* or *moras*, sounds and characters which we approximate with western syllables.

The poems in this book use each *haiku's* words in sequence vertically, beginning each line. Japanese characters in traditional *haiku* are also written vertically though of course our English translations appear in phrases in the familiar horizontal form, often but not always using 5, 7 and 5 syllables.

In the 9th century what we call *haiku* today was written as the first part of a progressive formal poem called a *renga* or *tanka*. In a *renga* one person would start by writing the first three lines (5-7-5 *moras*) then another would add to it (7-7 *moras*) and alternating forms, a very long poem of linked verses would be composed by many writers. In the 16th century the first three lines began to be written separately and these short poems were called *hokku*.

The best known masters of *hokku* are Basho, Issa, and Buson, followed in the 19thcentury by, among others, Shiki, Soseki and Akutagawa. At the end of the 19th century Masaoka Shiki changed the name of this short poem form from *hokku* to *haiku*—and that's the name we know it by today.

Traditional *haiku* reflects the seasons. It also contains what the Japanese call a *kireji* or "cutting word", a change in direction, usually at the end of the poem, that surprises. We might call it a turn today, something often used in western poetry, and it's easy to see that the kireji or turn as well as the classic *haiku's* compression has parallels in the sonnet.

ADDITIONAL ACKNOWLEDGEMENTS

The *haiku* translations used for the poems in this book are drawn from a number of sources, some with no found attribution. Fortunately many *haikus* here came from the deeply considered translations by Robert Hass. His book, *The Essential Haiku*, which Hass edited and translated contains the writings and verses of Basho, Buson and Issa. His translations express better than any I have read, the essence and distinct character of each poet in the context of their time. Reading the book and the poets in it is a moving and transformative experience—an immersion in the essential haiku.

The haiku translated by Robert Hass appeared in: *The Essential Haiku: Versions of Basho, Buson, Issa*, edited by Robert Hass (The Ecco Press; 1995, 2012) and are reprinted by permission of The Ecco Press.

Special thanks to Wakako Suzuki. Using English translations, she ferreted out each of the masters' *haiku* in their original Japanese paying close attention to their essence. Together she compared the original with its the English counterpart to make sure the meanings corresponded.

And finally more personal thanks to David St. John, Dorothy Barresi and Richard Garcia, friends and immeasurably generous mentors who have given my work their time and thought. Invaluable too are my workshop partners, Keven Bellows, Mary Fitzpatrick, Kate Hovey, Candace Pearson, Beth Ruscio, Cathie Sandstrom, Carine Topal, Lynne Thompson and Brenda Yates, who have helped me to consider and weigh each poem's nuances, strengths and failings. I am endlessly grateful to you all.

Judith Pacht's *Summer Hunger* (Tebot Bach), won the 2011 PEN Southwest Book Award for Poetry, and her three triolets *The Year of the Heart (and the House)* was one of three winners in the 2017 Triolet/Rondeau Contest. Her chapbooks *User's Guide and St. Louis Suite* were published by Finishing Line Press, and her first chapbook and poetry collection, *Falcon*, was published by Conflux Press.

A three-time Pushcart nominee, Pacht was first place winner in the Georgia Poetry Society's Edgar Bowers competition. Her work has appeared in journals that include *Ploughshares, Runes, Nimrod* and *Phoebe*, and her poems were translated into Russian where they were published in *Foreign Literature* (Moscow, Russia). Her work appears in numerous anthologies.

Pacht recently read at the Los Angeles Times Festival of Books, at Charleston's Piccolo Spoleto Festival and has read and taught Political Poetry at Denver's annual LitFest at the Lighthouse.

She lives in Los Angeles with her partner, Kenneth Fisher.